T0285331

I F*CKED YOU IN MY SPACESHIP

Louis Emmitt-Stern

I Fucked You in My Spaceship was first performed at VAULT Festival, London, on 7 February 2023. The production subsequently transferred to Soho Theatre, London, on 19 June 2023.

I FUCKED YOU
IN MY SPACESHIP

by Louis Emmitt-Stern

CAST

LEO	**Jonas Moore**
DAN	**Max Hyner**
AL	**Felix Kai**
ANNA	**Fanta Barrie**
EMILY	**Lucy Spreckley**
ROBERT	**Jacob Bukasa**

CREATIVE TEAM

Director	**Joseph Winer**
Lighting Designer	**Abi Turner**
Sound Designer	**Bella Kear**
Movement Director	**Patrice Bowler**
Producer	**Katy McLeod**
Stage Manager	**Natalya Scase**

CAST

Jonas Moore | LEO

Training: LAMDA. Theatre credits include *I Fucked You in My Spaceship* (VAULT Festival), and three consecutive Edinburgh Fringe plays with Limerence Productions. Film/TV include *Surviving Christmas with the Relatives* with Julian Ovenden and Sally Phillips, and Steven Spielberg and Tom Hanks' WWII miniseries *Masters of the Air*. He plays Captain Frank D. Murphy, whose memoir Jonas subsequently narrated.

Max Hyner | DAN

Training: Guildford School of Acting. Professional credits include *Ankle Swingers* (Omnibus Theatre), *I Fucked You in My Spaceship* (VAULT Festival), *Dickie Must Die* (Etcetera Theatre), the short film *We Should Do This Again Some Time*, *Macbeth* and *The Merry Wives of Windsor* (Pendley Shakespeare Festival). Credits whilst training include *Better than Death*, *Babe the Sheep Pig*, *Three Sisters*, and *Romeo and Juliet*.

Felix Kai | AL

Training: Royal Central School of Speech and Drama. Felix recently guest starred in *Midsomer Murders*. His stage credits include *I Fucked You in My Spaceship* (VAULT Festival), and *DREAM SCHOOL* (The Space). Their credits whilst training include *The Duchess of Malfi*, *The Castle*, *Threepenny Opera*, and the European Premiere of *promiscuous/cities*. As a writer, Felix has worked with Royal Court Theatre, Kiln Theatre, Soho Theatre, and Objective Fiction.

Fanta Barrie | ANNA

Training: Rose Bruford College. Theatre credits include *Seeds* (No Stone Theatre), *The Ministry of Lesbian Affairs* (Soho Theatre), *Belly Up* (Turbine Theatre), *The Lovely Bones* (Birmingham Rep & UK Tour), *The Cereal Cafe* (The Other Palace), *The Amber Trap* (Theatre503), *Songlines* (HighTide). Radio credits include *The Future of Radio* (BBC Radio 3), *Life Sentence* (Mags Creative), *The Fall Down* (BBC 4). TV credits include *Kitty in My Lady Jane* (Amazon Prime)

Lucy Spreckley | EMILY

Lucy is an actor and voice-over artist. Recent credits include *I Fucked You in My Spaceship* (VAULT Festival), *The Real* (Cockpit Theatre), *Little Red Riding Hood* (UK Tour), *Everything Between Us* (Marylebone Theatre), and Janet on the UK tour of *The Rocky Horror Experience*.

Jacob Bukasa | ROBERT

Training: Mountview Academy of Theatre Arts.

Jacob is a recent graduate whose credits include commercial projects for McDonald's and the NHL, and the short film *Whatever It Takes* (London Film Academy). Credits whist training include *Macbeth, Awake and Sing, Off The Endz* and *Twelfth Night*.

CREATIVE TEAM

Louis Emmitt-Stern I Writer

Louis is an award-winning writer and director from Gibraltar based in London. His debut play *Slippery* won Soho Theatre's Tony Craze Award in 2021.

I Fucked You in My Spaceship won an Origins Award for Outstanding New Work at VAULT Festival 2023, following its critically acclaimed sold-out premiere. Louis was called 'a rising star playwright' by Time Out. The play subsequently transferred to Soho Theatre, London.

Louis' other work has been performed at Watford Palace Theatre, Southwark Playhouse, The Pleasance Theatre Islington, LAMDA, Ivy Arts Centre, and supported by Farnham Maltings. He trained at Guildford School of Acting, and the Royal Central School of Speech and Drama, and is an alumnus of the Gibraltar Academy of Music and Performing Arts, Soho Theatre Writers Lab, Soho Writers Alumni Group, National Theatre Young Playwrights Programme, and Young Lyric Directors Course at Lyric Hammersmith.

Louis was a finalist for an HM Government of Gibraltar Cultural Award for his production of Duncan Macmillan's *Lungs*, and for his work with young people in the arts and education. He teaches acting and playwriting both in the UK and Gibraltar.

Joseph Winer I Director

DIRECTOR: *I Fucked You in My Spaceship* (VAULT Festival), *Don't Smoke in Bed* (VAULT Festival), *Drag Baby* (King's Head Theatre), *The Happy Prince* (Watford Palace/Imagine Watford), *Breeding* (Watford Palace/Swings & Roundabouts), *My Shitty but Romantic First Time* (XPOSED, Southwark Playhouse), *Pictland* (Katzpace/Watford Fringe), *MEDEA* (Pinter Studio, Queen Mary Theatre Company).

DRAMATURG; *Housewerk* (Arcola Theatre Queer Collective). ASSISTANT DIRECTOR: *Scab* (Arcola/VAULT Festival), *Hamlet* (Iris Theatre), *Wild About Phones* (Imagine Watford).

Joseph is Artistic Director of PackPack Theatre Company, an alumnus of Soho Theatre Writers' Lab (Tony Craze Longlist), and recipient of the Sunday Times Harold Hobson Drama Critic Award. He has also directed 30+ productions with young people and community companies, including plays, pantomimes and musicals.

Abi Turner | Lighting Designer

Abi Turner is a neurodivergent and queer lighting designer and accessibility consultant. They graduated with a First-Class Honours Degree in Lighting Design from Rose Bruford College in 2020.

LIGHTING DESIGNER: *It's a Motherf**king Pleasure* (Soho Theatre & VAULT Festival), *Operation Hummingbird* (York Theatre Royal), *Pressure Drop*, *When This is Over* (The Yard Theatre), *Savage Heart* (Pleasance Downstairs, Norwich Puppet Theatre, & Sheffield Drama Studio), *Surfacing* (VAULT Festival), *A Monster Calls* (The Watermill Theatre*), How Disabled Are You?* (Omnibus Theatre & Park Theatre), *A Partnership* (Kings Head Theatre & Regional Tour), *Essentially Black* (Soho Theatre & Camden People's Theatre), *When Rachel Met Fiona* (The Space).

ASSISTANT LIGHTING DESIGNER: *Henry V* (Donmar Warhorse).

ASSOCIATE LIGHTING DESIGNER: *Milk and Gall* (Theatre503).

Abi's access work specialises in Relaxed Performances. They have consulted for companies including Flawbored, Theatre503, ASYLUM Arts, and worked in association with the National Theatre and TourettesHero.

Bella Kear | Sound Designer

Bella graduated from LAMDA in July 2021 with a First-Class Honours Degree in Production and Technical Arts.

SOUND DESIGNER: *Invisible* (Bush Theatre & Brits Off-Broadway), *Clutch*, *Elephant*, *The Kola Nut Does not Speak Englis*h (Bush Theatre), *The Animal Kingdom* (The Hampstead), *The Night Woman* (The Other Palace), *First Love is the Revolution* (E15), *The Faith Machine* (RADA), *The Last of the Pelican Daughters*, *Education, Education, Education* (ArtsEd), *Darling* (Hope Theatre).

ASSOCIATE SOUND DESIGNER: *Newsies* (Troubadour Wembley Park), *Seven Methods of Killing Kylie Jenner* (Swedish Transfer), *Purple Snowflakes and Titty Wanks* (Royal Court), *Blue/Orange* (Theatre Royal Bath), *A Place For We* (Park Theatre).

Patrice Bowler | Movement Director

Patrice is a multi-disciplinary artist hailing from the west coast of British Columbia. Recent movement directing credits include *I Fucked You in My Spaceship* (VAULT Festival), *Les Filles Du Roi* (Raven Theatre/Fugue Theatre*), The Annual Walk of Terror* (Caravan Farm Theatre), *Stories*

That Transform Us (Urban Ink), *Forty-Seven, Take Care* (Here For Now Theatre Festival). She has worked as a puppeteer on two parallel productions where giant sea goddess puppets educated the audience on the urgent topic of ocean health and climate change: *Sedna* (Urban Ink/ Caravan Farm Theatre), and *Storm* (Vision Mechanics).

Katy McLeod | Producer

Katy is a freelance Producer, Churchill Fellow and Access Support Worker, who is currently Associate Producer for Cast, a theatre in Doncaster. Katy has worked in producing teams on projects with the Birmingham Repertory Theatre, nabokov Theatre Company, Watford Palace Theatre and with Roundhouse Resident Artists. She has also presented shows at Latitude Festival, Camden Roundhouse, and produced a project as a part of the Barbican Open Lab. Katy is passionate about accessibility and diverse representation on stage and behind the scenes.

Natalya Scase | Stage Manager

Natalya is a stage and production manager from South Wales. She trained at the Guildhall School of Music and Drama, graduating with a BA (Hons) in Technical Theatre. As a freelancer, Natalya has worked at Hampstead Theatre, The Barbican, and Wilton's Musical Hall. Other previous credits include *Super High Resolution* (Soho Theatre), *LOL Surprise Live!* (UK & European Tour), and *Handa's Surprise* (Little Angel Theatre). She is currently resident deputy production manager for the Unicorn Theatre.

SOHO THEATRE is London's most vibrant producer for new theatre, comedy and cabaret. Opened in 2000, bang in the creative heart of London, it is one of the country's busiest venues with a buzzing bar and a year-round festival programme with a queer, punk, counter-culture flavour. Work extends far beyond its home with a UK and international touring programme and connections; presenting shows and scouting talent at Edinburgh Festival Fringe plus close links with the Melbourne International Comedy Festival. Soho Theatre is UK's leading presenter of Indian comedians from the burgeoning scene there and have partnerships and a Soho Theatre Comedy Producer based in Mumbai.

Soho Theatre produces and co-produces new plays, works with associate artists and presents the best new emerging theatre companies and comedians. It presents the early work of countless UK artists (many who become industry giants) and presents many international artists' London debuts. It has a thriving variety of artist and talent development programmes, artists under commission and in development, and two new writing awards including the Tony Craze Award for its Writers' Lab participants and the national Verity Bargate Award for new playwrights.

Soho Theatre is working towards the 2024 opening of an exciting new second London venue, **Soho Theatre Walthamstow**. A culmination of many years of Soho's work, in collaboration with a grassroots local campaign, to save a glorious, 1930's art deco venue with an incredible heritage reinvented as a 1,000-capacity venue for world-class comedy, panto, performance and participation – a 'local theatre with a national profile'.

I FUCKED YOU IN MY SPACESHIP

Louis Emmitt-Stern

Acknowledgements

I love reading play acknowledgements. There is something brilliantly investigatory, almost intrusive, that makes me feel like a detective... or a spy. Peeking into the inner world of the making of a show. Piecing together the story of the people who made it happen. In this case, I am fortunate there are so many of these people. I am beyond grateful for all of them. If you're investigating these acknowledgements for similar reasons, then I hope you enjoy uncovering their brilliant contributions as much as I have enjoyed working with them.

First and foremost, thank you to Joseph Winer for your astounding instincts, your inclusive and kind approach, and for facilitating this text so delicately from page to stage. Thank you for carrying this play to the finish line, and occasionally carrying me too.

A huge thank you to #TeamSpaceship at VAULT Festival and Soho Theatre. Jonas Moore, Max Hyner, Felix Kai, Lucy Spreckley, Rebecca Banatvala, Lewis Shepherd, Fanta Barrie, and Jacob Bukasa, Bella Kear, Laura Howard, Abi Turner, Patrice Bowler, Caelan Oram, Megha Dhingra, Clarice Montero, and Katy McLeod. Thank you for your creativity, your laughter, and your openness. Mostly, thank you for your friendship.

Bec Martin, Andy George, Kate Tregear, and the team at VAULT Festival 2023.

Gill Greer, Lakesha Arie-Angelo, Jules Haworth, David Luff, Adam Brace, Dimple Pau, Rose Abderabbani, Hannah Andrews, Augustin Wecxsteen, Damian Regan, and everyone at Soho Theatre. Thank you for holding me up, giving me a home as a writer, and championing my work.

My friends and collaborators who lent their voices to the first and second readings of this play in development. Teague

Selmon, Tom Baker, Joseph Saunders, Chloe Bradbury, Kirsty Dymond, Luke Bromley, and subsequently Lydia Piper, Imogen Redpath, Michael Elias, Rhys Speight, Nina Frantzekaki, and Seb Flatau.

The Hon Prof John Cortes, Seamus Byrne, Davina Barbara, HM Government of Gibraltar Ministry for Culture, and Gibraltar Cultural Services. Thank you for your continuous support.

John Fitzpatrick, Jennifer Farmer, Laura McCluskey, Clare Bayley, Nathan Ellis, Leo Butler, and Mark Boutros. Thank you for your mentorship, your notes, your encouragement, and for making me a better writer.

Maddie Hindes, Matt Applewhite, Robin Booth, Sarah Liisa Wilkinson, Deborah Halsey, and all at Nick Hern Books.

My wonderful agent Maddie O'Dwyer. Thank you for taking care of my wellbeing alongside my writing, and always putting me back together whenever I fall apart.

Mum and Dad. I couldn't do any of it without you. Thank you.

L.E.S. (2023)

I Fucked You in My Spaceship was first performed at VAULT Festival, London, on 7 February 2023, with the following cast:

LEO	Jonas Moore
DAN	Max Hyner
AL	Felix Kai
ANNA	Rebecca Banatvala
EMILY	Lucy Spreckley
ROBERT	Lewis Shepherd
Director	Joseph Winer
Lighting Designer	Laura Howard
Sound Designer	Bella Kear
Movement Director	Patrice Bowler
Stage Manager	Caelan Oram
Casting Associates	Megha Dhingra
	Clarice Montero

Characters

LEO
DAN, *his boyfriend*
AL, *a stranger*
ANNA
EMILY, *her girlfriend*
ROBERT, *a student*

Characters can be any race.

Setting

Leo, Dan, and Al's story takes place in Leo and Dan's apartment, and a nearby café.

Anna, Emily, and Robert's story takes place in Anna and Emily's apartment.

Both stories take place in the same universe, orbiting the same sun, and in doing so, orbit one another.

Note on Text

This play is written to be performed on a bare stage. There should be no scenery, no mime, no props, and no furniture unless explicitly stated.

Blackouts between scenes should be avoided.

(/) indicates the point of interruption in overlapping dialogue.

(…) indicates trailing off.

(–) indicates interruption. Within speech it indicates a break in syntax.

(,) on a separate line indicates deliberate silence from pressure, expectation or desire to speak.

Lines in [square brackets] are unspoken, indicating an unfinished thought.

Punctuation is used freely and artistically to suggest delivery, not to conform to grammatical rules.

This text went to press before the end of rehearsals and so may differ slightly from the play as performed.

Prologue

Space. The Final Frontier.

The main theme from 2001: A Space Odyssey (*1968*) *plays.*

Heavy breathing begins to overlap. Like an astronaut in a space helmet. It gets louder and more sexual.

The music is about to reach its crescendo when... Everything stops.

One

LEO *and* DAN.

LEO	Sorry just a minute sorry
DAN	Am I doing something / wrong?
LEO	No it's good it's Maybe the voice
DAN	The voice?
LEO	Not quite the same.
DAN	I'm sweating Going to get / some water.
LEO	It's a little more gentle, really If you watch the YouTube clips, the voice is more gentle
DAN	I was being gentle.
LEO	Okay okay yes sure.
	But,
	No. Not really.
	You were going for more of a 'husky' thing
DAN	I don't think so
LEO	A little too husky
	And I know that's part of it
DAN	That's not really…
LEO	When you're in the moment and you're inside me and saying my name

           and it's heavy breathing
           it's husky it's

DAN   Hard to breathe in the costume

LEO   But if you listen to the clip it's much more gentle
           And I understand why you'd think that

           because,
           You know,
           There's a prejudice…
           no not prejudice,
           a sort of…
           stereotype.
           Yes.
           Isn't there.

DAN   Is there?

LEO   That's husky – not husky not… just all
           'GRAHHHH' and like
           aggressive
           and
           violent
           and

DAN   I'm not being violent.

LEO   No no,
           No.
           Of course you're not
           But to some extent you've got this predetermined
           idea that they're violent
           and that's not your fault. Its the media, really,

           But it's about recognising that it's only
           a stereotype
           And most aliens
           Once you get past that
           Are actually quite gentle and peaceful
           And I think if you rewatch the YouTube clip
           you'll get that

	Because I want to believe you. Like fuck me, you know. Like you've abducted me and you're fucking me in your spaceship And that's hot. And I'm there, I'm almost there And I think if the voice was a little more gentle It'd be like fireworks Don't you think?
DAN	…
LEO	?
DAN	,
	Can we try it without the costume?
LEO	Don't you think if –
	What?
DAN	I'll do the voice
LEO	You don't want to wear the costume?
DAN	It's a million degrees
LEO	It's the most important bit
DAN	Can't you imagine it?
LEO	Imagine you wearing the costume?
DAN	Sure
LEO	But that's the point of the costume. So I can imagine you / as the alien
DAN	Yes, I know the point of the costume,
LEO	Otherwise I'm imagining you wearing the costume imagining you as the alien. And that's too many steps
DAN	I'll wear it.
LEO	Well, no…

DAN   Sorry?

LEO   You have to *want* to wear it
         Otherwise it's not sexy it's not

DAN   It's *your* fantasy

LEO   No of course, but
         If you don't want it, I mean, to some extent,
         Well, it's a bit fucking weird, isn't it?

DAN   I do I do

LEO   You're just a guy in an alien costume.

DAN   I'm putting it on

LEO   No actually

         Because it's not just the costume
         It's the voice
         And a bunch of other things and

DAN   What other things?
         A *bunch*?

LEO   Let's have, you know,
         some normal sex,

DAN   I can do it

LEO   Let me finish,
         We can try this again and you can be 'you'
         Because you're very good at that,
         And then maybe...
         ...we don't have to...
         ...But if you didn't want to play the alien

DAN   I can

LEO   Yes I know baby of course you can but
         If you didn't *want* to
         We can get someone else to be the alien
         Someone we know
         Or don't know

	That's entirely up to us really. Someone with a gentle voice And they can do that, And they can wear the costume.
DAN	Get someone else involved?
LEO	For the alien stuff.
DAN	I don't know if I want to do that.
LEO	Okay, that's okay, that's
DAN	No. I don't think... no. , Who do you have in mind?
LEO	That's something we'd / talk –
DAN	No one from the office.
LEO	, If you don't want that, okay.
DAN	You don't think it would be awkward?
LEO	If you think it would be awkward, I can understand that.
DAN	You've got someone in mind. From the office.
LEO	I didn't say that.
DAN	You do. You fucking do.
LEO	No, of course not But , Well, I mean, We know Ryan's into that stuff.
DAN	Ryan from HR, Ryan?

LEO   He posted those photos
            The ones from Comic Con
            On Instagram.

            ,

            And his voice

DAN   Nothing like the clip.

LEO   No, sure, but Potentially.
            It's got potential.

DAN   ,

            What would I do?
            If I'm not the alien.

LEO   What would you like?

DAN   I'll think about it.

LEO   Of course.

            ,

            And if you didn't want to be involved

            ,

            You wouldn't have to be there. If you didn't want
            to.

            ,

            I'll send Ryan the clip, see what he thinks.

Two

ANNA *and* EMILY.

ANNA	It's just a bit of a nightmare.
EMILY	Do you think?
ANNA	Nightmare to spell, really.
EMILY	I don't know.
ANNA	I'm dyslexic / basically.
EMILY	No you're not.
ANNA	Want to be able to spell my kid's name
EMILY	Not that difficult.
ANNA	Don't want people to struggle To spell it.
EMILY	Fuck those people.
ANNA	No. Of course. Fuck those people. Of course. But like, what about her? Always getting your name mis-spelt. At school. On autographs. It's a bit of a faff.
EMILY	Niamh (?)
ANNA	Don't want to do that to our child.
EMILY	I've crossed it out.
ANNA	I think that's best.
EMILY	I've got Bernadette on the 'maybe' list.
ANNA	Bernadette?
EMILY	It's vintage.
ANNA	It's fucking catholic that's what it is.
EMILY	It's on the maybe list.

ANNA   I'm not carrying a Bernadette
            I'm not getting itchy skin and bleeding gums and
            swollen ankles for a Bernadette.

EMILY   Crossing out Bernadette.

ANNA   'Is that your daughter?
            'Oh lovely
            'What's her name again? 'Bernadette?'

EMILY   At least if it's a boy /

ANNA   Could you imagine that? /

EMILY   If it's a boy at least we've settled on that.

ANNA   Right.

EMILY   We're decided.

ANNA   That's a big word.

EMILY   Thought we'd

ANNA   I'm very keen on it.
            Keen, I think is the word. Keen.

EMILY   What's wrong with it?

ANNA   Nothing's wrong with it.

EMILY   We like it. We like Eddie.

ANNA   (*To herself.*) 'Eddie'

EMILY   We love Eddie

ANNA   Not sure if it's really got
            Much

            ,

            Sex appeal.

EMILY   Eddie Izzard, Eddie Murphy
            Eddie Redmayne,

ANNA   Yes
            Yes of course

EMILY   More sex appeal than Eddie fucking Redmayne?

ANNA   I get that.
             I do, but

EMILY   Edward Cullen.

ANNA   Don't think that's... He's a character.
             Characters don't count.

EMILY   Ed Norton, Eddie Cibrian

ANNA   Ed Sheeran.

EMILY   ,

             Oh.

             ,

ANNA   Exactly.

EMILY   Oh no.

ANNA   Yeah.

EMILY   We can't do that.

ANNA   That's what I thought.

EMILY   Crossing out Ed.

ANNA   Do you think maybe...

EMILY   I've crossed it out.

ANNA   Do you think maybe we're not ready?

EMILY   ,

             No.
             I don't think that.
             Why? Do *you* think that?

ANNA   I don't know.

EMILY   I think, yes, we're ready.
             We both said.

ANNA   If we can't decide on a name

EMILY   Don't start this.

ANNA   I'm not.

EMILY   Don't get all...
           Indecisive-y now.
           It's not a real feeling. You know this.
           Always do this when you're scared.

ANNA   I've had this idea In my head
           Ever since I was little
           I carried a pillow under my top and walked
           around the living room

           And wrapped up my teddy-unicorn in blankets
           Making her little bottles of milk

           Had this idea in my head for I don't know how
           long

           Scared of ruining that.

EMILY   We're just making a list.
           That's all we're doing.

ANNA   Yes.

EMILY   Look.
           A list.
           That's all it is.
           A piece of paper.

           We don't have to make any decisions.

ANNA   I know.

EMILY   Maybe
           And we'll look at their face
           Into their little eyes
           And we'll know.

ANNA   Do you think?

EMILY   People say that.
           They say
           We just saw him or her or them and
           We knew.

ANNA   What if I don't know?
              What if I look down at my baby and I don't know
              who they are.
              Just some... entity
              Alien to me
              Staring back.
              A nothing.

              Or worse,
              Look down and all I see is Ed Sheeran.

EMILY   I think you're overthinking this.

ANNA   Written across his forehead in big black letters.
              I don't know if I'm ready for that.

EMILY   ,

              What do you want to do?

ANNA   I don't know.

              Let's put it all under the maybe list
              And come back to it.

              Just keep it there
              Baby
              As a 'maybe'
              Until we're sure.

Three

LEO *and* DAN.

DAN	It's a lot to digest.
LEO	Is it?
DAN	For Ryan.

It's quite a lot to put onto him.
Quite a big sort of
Gesture
I suppose

LEO   Well

DAN   Because we've got to go to work.
Have you thought about that?

If he says no
We've got to go to work with him
And he'll
We'll all have this
Thing
This gesture that's been made
Especially
If he says no

Or if he says yes.

What if he says yes?

He says yes
And he comes over.
And then we go to work

Every day

And chat through the sales reports
Like absolutely / nothing's…

LEO   Okay

DAN   Do you see what I'm / saying?

LEO   I think so.

DAN	It's worth thinking about
LEO	Absolutely I hear you, baby.
DAN	Thank you.
LEO	And I guess I'm not really thinking about these things I'm not really worried because I didn't really think he would be You know That he'd be awkward about it.
DAN	No.
LEO	He's very professional.
DAN	No, of course.
LEO	I wasn't just going to come out with it. I wasn't just going to say: Hello Ryan. I hope you're well. Little opportunity for you Would you like to come round sometime this week and pretend to be an alien?
DAN	No / no I know.
LEO	Is Wednesday any good? Wednesday or Thursday works well for us. Let me know. My very best wishes, Leo.
DAN	Of course not.
LEO	Just going to feel him out. At first. Just feel See if I get a... You know A vibe.

DAN   Do we know him well enough?
           Like that?
           A *vibe*?
           We don't really know him.

LEO   I know him.

DAN   Not really.

LEO   If you don't want to do this

DAN   I do.

LEO   Hey hey
           I don't want you to feel pressured

DAN   I don't.
           No.
           I want to.

LEO   Okay.

DAN   Been having a look.
           As an idea.
           This website.

LEO   Oh?

DAN   You can post an ad

LEO   Online?

DAN   Make a profile or something.
           See?

           And there's a box where you can write things.
           What you're looking for.
           What you're not looking for.

LEO   A stranger?

DAN   We don't have to reply.

           We can put it out there

           And if we get someone we don't like
           We can ignore them.

Four

ANNA *and* ROBERT.

ANNA   Haven't decided who we are taking forward yet.

ROBERT   Oh.

ANNA   We're just meeting people at the moment.

ROBERT   So is this like an interview, or…?

ANNA   No,
            Oh no.
            That's very…
            No.
            More like a chat, really.

ROBERT   Okay.

ANNA   We just want to sort of see what kind of person
            you are.
            We want you
            Not you
            Whoever
            Maybe you
            To be involved

ROBERT   Involved?

ANNA   I mean, not *involved* involved

ROBERT   What level of involved are we talking?

            If you need someone to pop round and play
            a couple of games
            I can do that.
            I can do Lego.

            But if it's a financial involvement

ANNA   No no

ROBERT   I'm pretty broke.
            That's basically why I'm here.

ANNA   We're not asking for any money.
            Nothing like that.

ROBERT	Okay.
ANNA	Just Being Present.
	Whenever you want to.
ROBERT	Not that big a deal, right?
	I can understand why it's a big deal for *you*, but
	I've just got to go in there. Do my thing.
	That's all, really (?)
ANNA	We want him or her them We want them to know about their father. Not just at eighteen. But throughout.
	That's the problem with the sperm bank. You're not allowed to know.
ROBERT	Of course
ANNA	It's all anonymous
ROBERT	Yes
ANNA	Not really how we 'envisioned' Is that the right word? 'envisioned' it. Not what we wanted, really. So we're interviewing Chatting Chatting with people Like this.
	It's a chat.
ROBERT	Great.
ANNA	Nicer for you. Can't imagine what it must be like

Donating your…
Your…
Seed (?) /
And

ROBERT   Seed?

ANNA   Then leaving and never knowing.
Walking around
Walking to the shops
Sitting on the bus and maybe
The kid sat next to you
Maybe that kid's yours.
Imagine that.

ROBERT   That doesn't bother me too much.
It's mainly the money.

ANNA   Drive myself crazy imaging that.

ROBERT   They don't give you much.
At the clinic.
For a go.
Barely covers the Uber there and back.

Bit more money if you do it privately.

ANNA   Robert, right? Your name.

ROBERT   Yes.
Robert.

ANNA   Robert. Great. Robert.
Sorry
Double checking.
My fiancée, she does all the 'getting in contact'
and stuff.
Just on her way home.

ROBERT   Okay.

ANNA   Emily. She's the one you've been speaking to.
I'm Anna.
I'm the one you'll be inseminating.

ROBERT   Yes. She said.

ANNA   We'd need you to take some tests.
    If that's okay.

ROBERT   Right.

ANNA   Whoever we chose.
    We'd need to make sure they're clear.

ROBERT   Of course.

ANNA   ,

    (*To herself.*) Robert.

ROBERT   Yes?

ANNA   Oh no,

    I was just saying…

    Feeling how it sits on the tongue.

    'Robert'

    You know, Robert.

ROBERT   Right.

ANNA   We're thinking about names. For the baby.

    ,

    Lovely name, yours.
    Robert.

ROBERT   Do you think so?

ANNA   Don't hear it very often nowadays, do you?
    'Robert.'

ROBERT   Is your fiancée…?

ANNA   Any minute now, should be.

ROBERT   Great.

ANNA   Do you want some water, Rob?

ROBERT   No, thank you, I'm

ANNA   Sure?

ROBERT   Just Robert.

ANNA   Sorry?

ROBERT   I'm just Robert.
            Rob
            You said...

ANNA   For short (?)

ROBERT   Just Robert.

ANNA   Just Robert. I see I see.
            That's very respectable.

ROBERT   I think so.

ANNA   ,

            Not even your mum?

ROBERT   ?

ANNA   Does your mum call you Rob?

ROBERT   No.

ANNA   What did she call you, like, as a baby?

ROBERT   Robert.
            That's what she called me.
            When I was born
            And each time after that.

ANNA   Baby Robert?

ROBERT   Yes.

ANNA   Never really thought about a baby being called
            Robert.
            Sort of sounds like ribbit. You know. Like a frog.

ROBERT   Right.

ANNA	Not you. I don't mean you. Robert suits you.
ROBERT	Do I look like a frog?
ANNA	What I mean is It's a name you grow into.
	Robbie is a boy's name. Robert is a man.
	Suits you because you're a man, you know. You're a proper, fleshed out, real... juicy man... man.
	You know,
	Fleshed out.
	,
	Funny imagining it the other way round. A little baby Robert Walking around Oh look It's little baby Robert There he goes.
ROBERT	Fuck
ANNA	Little Robert with his little Robert feet and his little Robert water bottle.
ROBERT	Actually I'll have some water if that's
ANNA	Yes
ROBERT	Thanks
ANNA	Just going to give Emily /
ROBERT	Actually I might /
ANNA	Give her a call.
ROBERT	I might go. Sorry.

ANNA   What?

ROBERT   I don't know what…
            I don't normally do this kind of thing.

ANNA   No
            It's me.
            Being weird
            Have I ballsed this up?
            I've ballsed this up, haven't I.

ROBERT   Just don't think it's for me.

ANNA   Emily will be here any minute.
            She's much better at talking to people than me.

ROBERT   I'm really sorry.

ANNA   Okay
            Look,
            Okay

            Could we just
            Have a *Men in Black* moment
            Boop.
            Erase All Memory
            And just
            Give it another go?

ROBERT   I don't know.

ANNA   Look
            It'll be easy.

            Hi.
            I'm Anna.

ROBERT   …

ANNA   This is where you say 'I'm Robert'

ROBERT   Oh.
            Er

            Hi.
            I'm Robert.

ANNA   Lovely to meet you, Robert.

            ,

            Lovely name.

Five

LEO *and* AL.

LEO	Sprinkled chocolate on top.
	Suddenly thought
	I don't know if he even wants chocolate.
	And I was going to come back and ask
	But sort of just... panicked
	And
	Sprinkled
	The
	Chocolate
	On
	Is that okay?
AL	Erm
LEO	I always think
	Fuck it.
	It's Chocolate. Fuck it.
	At the end of the day it's a bit of chocolate
	Who doesn't like a bit of chocolate
AL	I don't.
LEO	Oh
AL	Yeah.
LEO	Really?
AL	I love chocolate, just
LEO	On a diet?
AL	Allergic.
LEO	Fuck.
AL	Quite badly.
LEO	Sorry
AL	You didn't know

LEO	I can scrape it off.
AL	Erm
LEO	Look, Look I'll just…
	scrape
	off
	the top
	Just take the top off the / …
AL	The froth /
LEO	Just like that.
	Ta dah.
	Can't even see it now.
AL	,
	Shouldn't really risk it.
LEO	No, Obviously. Shouldn't risk it.
AL	I'm sure it's fine, but…
LEO	No, of course.
AL	Get really bad.
LEO	Really?
AL	Patches.
LEO	Patches?
AL	One time I had to go to hospital
LEO	Shit.
AL	Actually stopped breathing.

LEO	Oh my god. Oh my god are you feeling okay? Do you feel okay now?
AL	Look at you.
LEO	Do you want to go to hospital in case? I can drive you.
AL	Look at your face. Gosh you're cute.
LEO	Huh?
AL	I shouldn't be laughing. This isn't funny I'm a cunt.
LEO	So you're not…
AL	God, no. Chocolate? I'd kill myself.
LEO	Oh Oh thank God. Jesus
AL	Didn't think you'd…
LEO	For a second I thought – Jesus, For a second, thought you were about to
AL	Didn't think you'd actually scrape it off. That's golden.
LEO	It's a bit of a mess.
AL	Breathe.
LEO	Okay.
AL	, So, You're 'horny human slave looking for sexy alien master'

LEO	Who?
	,
	Oh, right. Yes. That is, in fact, me, isn't it. Hello.
AL	Hi
LEO	My boyfriend wrote the ad. It's his account.
AL	Boyfriend?
LEO	He thinks he's very funny.
AL	There's two of you?
LEO	,
	Doesn't it say?
AL	Don't think so
LEO	On our profile. Pretty sure it says.
AL	Maybe I missed it.
	I mean I definitely missed it because…
LEO	Right.
AL	Boyfriend.
LEO	Is that… Does that make this difficult?
AL	It doesn't have to.
	We'd have to sort out the rules.
LEO	Rules?
AL	Set some boundaries. Just logistically What we're doing about that.

LEO	We know what we want. We know what we're looking for.
AL	Yes, Science / fiction
LEO	(*Whispering*.) Intergalactic – Sure.
AL	So I'm quite happy with that. Alien stuff
LEO	(*Whispering*.) Sure
AL	I'm a pretty open book Woosh. I'm there.
LEO	Great.
AL	I don't do shitting.
LEO	Oh.
AL	So if that's what you're looking for
LEO	No God no.
AL	There's nothing wrong with it.
LEO	No, Of course not. I'm sure there's not
AL	If that is your thing If that is what you're into
LEO	It's not. Why Why would you say that? My 'thing'?
AL	Not something to be ashamed about. Not how I wanted to come across.
LEO	No

AL	It's just not on the cards for me.
LEO	Me neither
AL	Okay.
LEO	It's not.
AL	I believe you.
LEO	Am I giving off a vibe?
AL	A vibe?
LEO	Yes.
AL	What vibe?
LEO	I don't know. Like I want to shit on your chest sort of vibe.
AL	I wasn't assuming…
LEO	No
AL	Just setting boundaries.
LEO	Okay.
AL	Apart from that I'm happy with most things.
	Obviously depending on where you come It's going to cost you more inside the arsehole But anywhere else It's pretty much a standard rate.
LEO	Sorry?
AL	So we'd have to *You'd* have to Decide that You know Amongst yourselves Beforehand

LEO	Could you just Rewind that a second
	Cost more?
AL	In the arse.
	But I don't know if The alien… If the costume has like a flap at the back or
	Do they? Aliens. Have assholes?
LEO	I think there's a misunderstanding
AL	Yes, Sorry. I'm sure their anatomy is very different
LEO	You seem lovely
	And you know You're fucking gorgeous
	So There's that.
	We're just… We're not looking for…
AL	Right.
LEO	Didn't know that this would be… That this is a paid thing.
	We just wanted something a bit more Casual.
AL	I understand.
LEO	Not that I'm… You know, Not that we're against it or anything. Hashtag support sex-workers and that.

AL   I don't normally do this kind of thing

            I saw your guys' profile and thought it looked fun.

LEO   Sure.

AL   Got to find a way somehow.
            Rising tuition fees, student living, the whole
            rhetoric.

LEO   You're a student?

AL   Second year.
            Engineering.

LEO   Engineering. Wow. Interesting.

            ,

            That's…

AL   Aeronautical Engineering.

LEO   Oh.

            ,

            Aeronautical.

            ,

            So that's like… / spaceships?

AL   Spacecraft,

            ,

            Yeah.

Six

EMILY *and* ANNA.

ANNA	It's called a conception cup.
EMILY	Right
ANNA	Got it from Boots.
EMILY	Looks… Fun.
ANNA	Fun?
EMILY	Interesting.
ANNA	Don't hold it like that.
EMILY	I'm not.
	Like what?
ANNA	Like it's a snotty tissue
EMILY	Keeping it clean. Don't want to dirty it. Fingerprints. Oils.
ANNA	Afterwards I've got to lie with my legs in the air apparently. That's what she says. On her blog.
EMILY	She's very…
ANNA	Really / good.
EMILY	Descriptive.
ANNA	There's more if you / scroll down.
EMILY	Oh look. There's a photo. She's included a photo.
ANNA	If you scroll past that. There's a bit For partners.

EMILY   A lot of photos.
          Quite intense.

ANNA   Most of it will drip out,
          That's what she says,

EMILY   Right.

ANNA   When I'm ready to stand up.

EMILY   So I've got to insert this / thingy, this…

ANNA   'Insert'?

EMILY   Conception cup,
          Into you,
          And then we wait?

ANNA   I can do it.

EMILY   You'll be on your back.

ANNA   Afterwards, yes.

EMILY   So shall I… hold it?
          Whilst you…

ANNA   That's okay.
          I know it makes you uncomfortable.

EMILY   I never said that.

ANNA   You just seem –

EMILY   I am very comfortable.

ANNA   Okay.

EMILY   ,

          Am I making *you* uncomfortable?

ANNA   It's started getting a bit…

EMILY   A bit…?

ANNA   Well, a bit…
          Clinical

EMILY   Clinical?

ANNA   'Insert'

EMILY   Sorry.

ANNA   Not a bad thing.
But if you don't know what to do,
If you don't know how to feel,
You don't have to pretend.
It's okay.

EMILY   I want to be here.
I want to be with you
Be part of it.

ANNA   You are, you're part of it
You're part of so much of it.
You will be.
The birth.
The coming home from the hospital.
The first steps. First words.
You're going to be part of all that.

But
I'm quite happy doing just this bit just me.

EMILY   ,

So, you want me to just...

,

Watch?

,

Like sit on the side and watch you?

ANNA   Well, no,
That's a bit creepy

EMILY   God, I feel like a man.
Is that what I am?
Am I a dad from the eighties?

ANNA   Stop it.

EMILY   I am
            I'm an eighties dad.

ANNA   Don't make me laugh

            I can't laugh with this in.
            It'll shoot back out

EMILY   No thank you.

ANNA   I'll come get you
            Once I'm done.

            Okay?

Seven

LEO *and* AL.

LEO	Got his arm up You know Like he's a flying. Like he's a superhero.
AL	He'll be dreaming.
LEO	You can have a look If you like
	Best not to wake him.
LEO	You're fine. He'll sleep through anything.
AL	Wouldn't want to ruin the dream.
LEO	Sometime I think I could be, You know, Murdered Actually being mutilated And he'll sleep through it.
	Worst superhero ever.
AL	Right.
	,
LEO	You can use any of those.
AL	Oh.
LEO	They're all clean in that pile, so
	,
	Except the purple one That's mine.
AL	Right.
LEO	Not *mine*. That sounded a bit…

It's not *my towel*.
I'm not possessive.
Just like using the purple one.

AL   Right.

LEO   Soft.

AL   Sure

LEO   You can use that one.
            If you want.
            There are other colours

AL   Was about to head off actually.
            Trying not to wake you.

LEO   No no,
            You didn't
            I was already awake.
            Would've waited anyway
            So by all means,
            If you fancy it

AL   That's okay.

LEO   Okay.

AL   ,

            Unless you want me to take a shower with you.
            If that's what you're asking.

LEO   Just meant
            It can get quite sweaty
            In the costume
            Just thought you might fancy one
            On your own

            Before you leave.

AL   If you'd like to watch
            If that's something you'd like
            Won't cost any more

LEO	(*Whispering*.) Oooh
	Oops.
	Ummm
	Sorry
	Bit loud.
	Don't want to wake Superman.
	Actually I'm
	I'm not saying anything to him.
	About the money.
	So
	If you could just, erm,
	If we can keep it like that.
AL	Between us.
LEO	Don't think he would really understand.
AL	You can pay in cash
	Next time
	If that's easier
	Harder to trace.
LEO	Next time?
AL	Oh.
	If there was something that wasn't…
LEO	No.
	Fuck.
	No no
AL	If it wasn't working
	If it
LEO	No,
	It did.
	It definitely did.
	Did you think so?
AL	I had fun.

LEO   Me too.

AL   You both seemed into it.

LEO   I was.
       I was, really

       And he was,
       You know

AL   Great.

LEO   I just
       I reckon it might just be a one-time thing.

AL   I understand.

LEO   You know,
       Like
       I had this
       We had this thing
       That we wanted to do
       And we did it
       Box ticked.

Eight

ANNA *and* ROBERT.

ANNA   ,

                  Everything
                  okay?

                  ,

                  Robert?

                          ROBERT   Yes
                                      I'm just –

                  Sorry
                  Making sure
                  you're
                  okay in there.

                  ,

                  Did you find it?

                  The lube
                  Can you see it?

                  ,

                  In the basket
                  by the sink.

                                      Yes, got it.

                  Good.
                  Good.

                  ,

                  Would you like
                  some music?

                                      What?

                  If you feel like
                  that would help.

                                   Could you
                                   just…

          Whatever's
          comfortable.

                                   Bit off-putting.
                                   Can't really…
                                   Whilst
                                   you're…

          Oh.
          Yes.
          Sorry.

                                   Keep losing my
                                   erection.

                                   Trying to stay
                                   in the mood.

          Of course.

                                   I'll let you
                                   know when

          No, no
          obviously.

          ,

          If there's
          anything you
          need
          you just let me
          know.

          ,

          There's a candle
          If that helps?

ROBERT   All done.

ANNA	Great. Wow. Fast.
ROBERT	Left it in there. On top of the toilet. Ready for you to...
ANNA	Thanks for doing this again.
ROBERT	No problem.
ANNA	Obviously it's quite expected
ROBERT	Sure
ANNA	To need to try a couple of times before it Before it sort of sticks (?) or whatever it does.
ROBERT	I don't mind. I'm very happy to.
ANNA	Thank you.
ROBERT	As many times as it takes.
ANNA	Not too many, I hope.
ROBERT	No. , Is Emily...?
ANNA	At work.
ROBERT	Back soon or?
ANNA	Academic conference. Late night for Emily.
ROBERT	Right.
ANNA	Probably best. Keep her busy. She's not very good with this side of things. She'll make a great mum once it's all done.

ROBERT   Of course.

ANNA   Should probably do my part now.
            Whilst everything is… fresh.

ROBERT   Can I stay?

ANNA   It's very boring.
            Lying on my back.
            Legs in the air.
            Nothing much to see, really.

ROBERT   Stay here
            As in,
            For a bit?

            ,

            As in…

            ,

            Just for the short term.

ANNA   Sorry
            Are you asking to move in?

ROBERT   Is that a bit forward?

            I wasn't really sure how to ask.

            I was hoping to ask when Emily was here, but,

ANNA   Move in with me and Emily?

ROBERT   I'm very clean.
            I don't smoke.

ANNA   God.

ROBERT   They're increasing my rent.
            Can't afford it.
            Even with the extra cash from this.
            Student loan only gets you so far.

            I noticed your spare room.

ANNA   The baby's room?

ROBERT   I'll be gone by then.
          Just somewhere for a few days
          Maybe a month.
          Time to sort myself out

ANNA   Right.

ROBERT   And I'll be here to help.
          With...
          We can do 'This'
          As much as you need.

ANNA   Listen, Robert.

          We really appreciate all your help.
          Everything you're doing to help us.
          We're very grateful.

          But living here?

          I don't think that's going to work.

          I'm sorry.

ROBERT   I understand.

ANNA   I can ask around, if you like.
          I'm sure we'll know someone.

ROBERT   Thank you.

ANNA   When do you need somewhere by?

ROBERT   ,

          Tomorrow.

ANNA   Oh.

          ,

ROBERT   It's late. I know.
          I only had the idea now
          In there
          Whilst I was...

          Popped into my head.
          Mid-way.

	Thinking This is a nice bathroom. I would be quite happy if this was my bathroom.
ANNA	Do you not have anyone you can stay with? Any family?
ROBERT	…
ANNA	,
	Fuck. Okay, erm
	,
	I'd have to talk to Emily.
ROBERT	Of course Yes, obviously.
	,
	And if she's okay with it?
ANNA	I don't know.
	I'd really need to talk to Emily first.

Nine

LEO *and* DAN.

DAN   If you wanted to do it again

LEO   Sorry?

DAN   Hypothetically
       If you wanted to.

LEO   Do you?
       Want to?
       Again.

DAN   I'm just talking hypothetically

LEO   Thought it was a one-time thing.
       Box ticked.

DAN   Me too.

LEO   A two-time thing?

DAN   If you wanted to.
       Or
       Something more regular, maybe.

       ,

       We don't have to

LEO   No, no
       I do
       I want
       I'm

       Glad.

DAN   Smiling.

LEO   Happy that you...

DAN   I love that smile.

LEO   You looked like you... [enjoyed]

DAN   I did.

LEO   You see what I mean?
            About 'The Approach'.
            He's just really got it.
            He wasn't trying to be too…
            Oooooo
            Look at me.
            I'm green.

            He was
            just
            very

DAN   Yes.

LEO   Intelligent.

DAN   I think he liked it.

LEO   So like,
            A regular thing?
            Like a regular Wednesday thing?

DAN   Doesn't have to be Wednesday.

LEO   No, of course.
            Just

DAN   Hypothetically.

LEO   Hypothetical Wednesdays.

DAN   Might not want to.
            Might have thought we were really fucking odd.

LEO   Do you think?

DAN   Blocked our number.
            Covered himself in tomato soup in the shower.

LEO   Was I too much?
            Was it the music?
            Do you think the music was too much?

DAN   Like with skunks.
            Removing the smell.

LEO	Skunks?
DAN	You know, In films.
LEO	…
DAN	It's a joke
LEO	Did I smell?
DAN	I'm joking. You smell great.
LEO	It's an expensive Jo Malone.
DAN	You smelt sexy.
LEO	, You think?
DAN	Very.
LEO	Okay. Okay cool. , I'll ask him. See when he's free. If he's free on Wednesdays.

Ten

ANNA *and* EMILY.

EMILY	Put him in the spare room for a few days Give him / time.
ANNA	A few *days*?
EMILY	Can't leave him on the streets Is that what you want / to do?
ANNA	Bit of an / exaggeration.
EMILY	Have him sleep in his car?
ANNA	Don't get me wrong I like the boy. He's interesting In his own way
EMILY	(*Whispering*.) He can hear you.
ANNA	He's going to be the father of our child. There's got to be some boundaries. I'm not sure I feel comfortable living with the father of my child.
EMILY	Okay so Let's Treat it like a trial period.
ANNA	A 'trial period'?
EMILY	See how it goes.
ANNA	We're putting him up, not employing him.
EMILY	You know what I'm saying.
ANNA	A trial period Sounds very…
EMILY	Not to his face Won't tell him that.
ANNA	Capitalist.

EMILY   See how he gets on.
            See how it works
            Him living here.

ANNA   Longer?

EMILY   See how it goes.

ANNA   Thought you said a few days.

EMILY   Just until the baby comes.
            You know what work's like.
            It's a lot of late nights for me at the moment.
            Might be nice to have someone here.
            Help sort things out.

ANNA   I'm fine.
            We're fine.

EMILY   Okay, if it doesn't work then...

            Right now, it's just a trial.

            Okay?

Eleven

DAN *and* AL.

DAN   Should be here any minute.

AL   If Wednesday isn't a good day...?

DAN   He's just in traffic.

AL   We can always change days.

DAN   Told him not to take the car.
I cycle in most days.
Avoid the traffic.

AL   Cyclist.

DAN   Wouldn't go that far.

AL   Cyclist legs.

DAN   ,

Do you think?

AL   They're nice.

DAN   Joined the environmental committee at sixth form
to help my UCAS.
Something extra-curricular
Ended up cycling to save the world.

AL   Does Leo cycle?

DAN   Don't tell him I told you, [but...]

He's scared of bicycles.
Never took the stabilisers off.
It's adorable really.

,

Can I get you anything?
Shouldn't be long now.

AL   Did you like school?

DAN   Got on with it, I suppose.
Like everyone else.

AL	You seem like the kind of person that did well at school.
	Academic.
DAN	Oh no. I was very average. Nothing special. Not like you Mr Aeronautical Engineer
AL	Mechanical.
DAN	What's that?
AL	I study mechanical engineering.
DAN	Oh. Sorry. I thought you did Aeronautical.
AL	That's okay. Easy mistake to make. They're all the same really.
DAN	What's that then? Mechanical?
AL	Whole bunch of things. Fridges. Gas turbines. Lifts. Escalators. , Bicycles.
DAN	Really?
AL	, Are you satisfied?
DAN	?
AL	With our arrangement.
DAN	You're very good at... I think you're great at what Leo wants.

AL	What about you? What do you want?
DAN	I normally come when he comes. I get off on him.
	It's his thing really. This.
AL	What's your thing?
DAN	As in…
	In the bedroom?
AL	Scenarios.
DAN	Don't think I have a 'thing'.
AL	Try me.
DAN	I'm vanilla. Honest. Nothing special.
AL	I won't laugh.
DAN	Wish I was more exciting.
	,
	I mean…
	,
	No.
AL	There. There it was.
DAN	No no.
AL	There's something there. I saw it. Just then. You stopped yourself. Go on.
DAN	,
	In school,
	The boys' changing room had this shower room.
	A wall with shower heads, in a row.
	After PE, we'd all get in.
	All the boys in this one room together.

Ahh this is bad
Sounds so cliché
Feel like…
A bad gay

,

Some of them would hurry to get dressed,
Or just not be thinking about it
Just talking and drying and changing
And they'd put their boxers back on before they
had dried themselves…
Their bodies still wet
And so
The boxers
They'd soak through quite quickly
And you could just see the outline

I always thought that was quite…

I think about that sometimes.

,

AL   I've still got my football kit from school.
            Bit mucky but
            I can bring it next week if you'd like?

            Would you like that?

Twelve

ROBERT *and* ANNA.

ROBERT   It's a pressure fit gate.

No screws or anything
Comes off whenever you want.
Can untighten it here
Same on the other side.

ANNA   Right.

ROBERT   You want them so the gate opens like this, away
from the door.

Put it on the other way round first
Kept bashing against it.

We'll have to buy the extension kit for the back
door because it's wider than eighty centimetres.
Anything wider than eighty centimetres you'll
need the extension kit

ANNA   Great, that's

ROBERT   On sale at John Lewis.
I can get some more
Put them on the doors downstairs if you like?

ANNA   This is great
Really
Thank you
But...

It's a bit early.
Don't you think?

ROBERT   Not really.

ANNA   I'm not even pregnant yet.
Don't want to jinx anything.

ROBERT   It'll happen before you know it
Suddenly there'll be a little thing
Crawling and walking all over the place

ANNA   I suppose

ROBERT   I didn't think I was going to be that fussed really.
            No offence.

            Now it's like…
            I'm going to have a baby in the world.
            Fuck. You know?

ANNA   Yes.

ROBERT   Everything feels a bit different.

            I've started having dreams. Is that weird?
            Having this dream that the baby keeps falling
            down the stairs
            Crawling out of that room
            On repeat.

            Woke up this morning and went to John Lewis
            and bought one of these.

            Make sure it's all safe.

ANNA   Great.
            That's great.
            And thank you, honestly Robert, thank you.
            And this is your house too
            We want you to feel like it's somewhere you
            can live.
            Happily.

            But also,
            It's our house.
            Do you see?

            Emily and I
            We've got a plan. How we want things to be.
            Once the baby comes

            Maybe next time
            Run it by us.
            Before you… you know.
            Gates.

ROBERT   Emily suggested it.

ANNA   ,

            Oh.

ROBERT   Told her about the dream.
            Last night.
            When she came home from work
            We had a few beers in the lounge.

            You'd already fallen asleep.

            She mentioned getting some gates.

            I thought I'd...
            Out my own pocket.
            A little thank you.

ANNA   Right.

            Well,
            Thank you.

ROBERT   Talked about some ideas I had for painting my
            room.
            For the baby.

ANNA   Painting?

ROBERT   Got some samples from B&Q. Tried them out on
            the wall over here.

            See?

            Emily thinks number two or three.

            What do you think?

ANNA   Erm
            Sorry
            Is that to paint the whole room?

ROBERT   Got some time on Friday.
            Hopefully get it done then.

            Have a sit with them.

Let me know.

,

We're leaning more towards number two at the moment.

Thirteen

LEO *and* DAN.

LEO	Twitter's popping off.
DAN	They're impressive, I'll give you that.
LEO	The photos aren't very good Just people driving past in their cars But you can sort of make it out.
DAN	Looks like there's quite a few
LEO	Three. Surely you can't make three in one night So that pretty much debunks / any
DAN	It could have been a group.
LEO	What?
DAN	Nothing. Would make sense if it was a group. Not just one bloke on his own in the middle of the night with a lawnmower.
LEO	Seem legit Look identical to the ones in Hull a couple months ago. Who's travelling down from Hull to hoax a crop circle? See Look at that.
DAN	I guess.
LEO	Should drive down before it gets dark.
DAN	Tonight?
LEO	Get some great shots on your camera. Way better than these.
DAN	Not tonight.
LEO	What?

DAN   He'll be here any minute.

LEO   Tell him we forgot.

DAN   It's Wednesday. It's always Wednesday.

LEO   He'll understand

DAN   Can't just cancel ten minutes before.
             He comes from Luton.

LEO   You know where he lives?

DAN   He told me he's started cycling in.

LEO   From Luton?

DAN   Don't want to let him down.
             It's rude.
             Especially for something that's not…

LEO   What?

DAN   Probably not real.

LEO   You don't think it's real?

DAN   I don't know.
             Do you?

LEO   I haven't seen it yet.

DAN   There'll be more next week.

LEO   Not like this.

DAN   I don't feel good about fucking him off to drive
             eighty miles into the middle of God knows where
             to take a picture of a circle in a field because
             someone on Twitter says so.

             I'm sorry.
             I think that's fair.

LEO   ,

             Okay.

             ,

DAN   Sorry if that…

LEO   I'm not really… 'in the mood' anyway.

DAN   Didn't mean to upset you.

LEO   Don't fancy having sex right now.

DAN   No, okay.

LEO   Thinking I'll run a bath.

DAN   I feel bad.

LEO   Don't.

DAN   ,

           I don't want to stop you.

           ,

           You go and see the crop circle.

           I'll stay here and wait for Al.

           ,

           You can still take my camera if you like?
           It's in my top drawer in the bedroom.

Fourteen

ANNA *and* EMILY.

EMILY	With the treatment there's a better chance it'll happen. That's what the doctor said.
ANNA	It won't.
EMILY	Said we can keep trying.
ANNA	She said it won't. That's what she was saying, really. Couldn't you hear it? Was listening to her and Felt like Failing Letting us down
EMILY	No
ANNA	Keep thinking That if I couldn't do this,
EMILY	Hey hey hey Deep breaths.
ANNA	No, I'm
EMILY	Come on, deep breath. , That's it. Another one. , Good. , If you want to keep trying… We can. I'm happy.
ANNA	Should still talk about it

EMILY   As long as it takes.

ANNA   Because it probably won't happen.
          Even if we keep trying / even if we…

EMILY   We don't know that.

ANNA   Okay.
          But,
          We do.

          We know.

EMILY   Anna

ANNA   No,
          No 'Anna'.
          No saying my name
          This is important.
          Because there's a lot of pressure on me if we
          don't talk about this.

EMILY   Okay.

ANNA   If we're going to keep throwing money at this.
          It's important to keep in mind that there are no
          guarantees.

          And if it doesn't work,
          The treatment,
          Where we go from there.

EMILY   ,

          There are other options, yes?

          ,

          We could adopt.

ANNA   No.

          ,

          Sorry I know you shouldn't say that. I know that
          makes me sound like an awful human being but
          I just

	don't want To do that.
	That's not how I wanted it.
EMILY	Okay.
	,
	I could try.
ANNA	,
EMILY	If we wanted to.
ANNA	You'd hate it.
EMILY	Just an idea.
ANNA	You hate maternity clothes.
EMILY	Not 'hate', just
ANNA	You think they're ugly and unflattering Which I always thought was a bit sexist actually but
EMILY	They are
ANNA	Of course they are But you don't say that out loud.
	And you don't like scans
EMILY	No.
ANNA	You think the jelly's too cold and reminds you of when you had a hernia.
EMILY	It does.
ANNA	You never wanted to carry. Every time we talk you say you can never see yourself…
EMILY	I didn't. But I talked to Robert / and –
ANNA	Robert?

EMILY   He suggested that
          Maybe
          If we wanted to …
          You know,
          Biologically,
          Then maybe it's our next best option.

ANNA   You told Robert?

EMILY   He's got to know.
          He's part of this.

ANNA   He suggested this then? Robert.

EMILY   He was very understanding.

ANNA   Great.

EMILY   And watching you both do it these past months
          It doesn't seem so scary any more.

          I know it's not how you planned it
          But if it means we get the nine months.
          We get the showers and the morning sickness and
          the hospital visits and the birth and the building it
          all together.

          And if you can't do it,
          At least you can be near it.

Fifteen

LEO *and* DAN. *Elsewhere,* **ANNA** *and* **EMILY.**

LEO   I fucked Ryan.

DAN   ,

LEO   Thought it would be best if I just came out with it
            Because
            I regret it.
            I do
            Of course.
            And

DAN   When?

LEO   Sorry?

DAN   When did you.

LEO   When? Erm,
            Yesterday.
            It's been eating away at me
            Eating
            Ever since
            Ever since we…

            I'm coming to you
            I'm here now
            I'm telling you straight away.
            Thought it would be better like this
            Straight away
            If I came to you.

EMILY   **A lot of bleeding**
            Didn't know what was happening.

ANNA   **Came straight from work.**

LEO   That's why I'm…

EMILY   **Quite scary**

LEO   Here.
            Now.

ANNA	**I'm here now.**
EMILY	**They did a scan.**
ANNA	**Okay, good, okay.**
	Good they did a scan.
EMILY	**Apparently quite normal** **Lots of women bleed at some point during** **pregnancy.** **That's what she said, the doctor.**
LEO	Dan?
ANNA	**No phone this week.** **The / conference.**
EMILY	**I know, conference.**
ANNA	**Can't have my phone on.**
EMILY	**No.**
LEO	My palms are sweating.
ANNA	**Should be there for you.** **Kept thinking about how scared you'd be** **All on your own.**
LEO	I can't keep things. Never had been able to
EMILY	**Well,** **Not on my own.**
LEO	Not that kind of person.
EMILY	**Robert came.**
LEO	Can't cover up things. Fucking hate it. Fucking hate the *pretending*.
DAN	I went to work today.
ANNA	**Did he?**

DAN	I had a meeting. With Ryan. This morning.
EMILY	**He was in his… working, In his room.**
DAN	I made a joke.
EMILY	**Offered to take me.**
DAN	Before we went in I made a joke about the water cooler.
ANNA	**Right.**
DAN	He laughed.
EMILY	**He had his car.**
DAN	Do you know how stupid that makes me feel?
LEO	I wanted to tell you sooner.
DAN	Probably thinking poor guy Not a fucking clue I've shagged his boyfriend I should probably laugh at his joke now. Throw a dog a bone.
LEO	He wouldn't have thought that.
ANNA	**Don't you think…**
LEO	He's very professional.
ANNA	**Me and you, should've been.**
EMILY	**Drove me there. Waited.**
ANNA	**Meant to be us.**
EMILY	**Sat in the car for hours Just to drive me back.**
LEO	I've thought this through a lot

EMILY   **Kept texting me.**
              Making sure I was okay. Inside.

LEO   How I want to say things

ANNA   **That's a bit...**

LEO   And everything's just slipping away right now
              Slipping out my brain.

ANNA   **Right. Okay.**

LEO   You got close with Al.
              I see it. Between you.
              Felt
              Removed
              Wanted you to feel it too, I guess.

EMILY   **Drove through McDonald's on the way back.**

DAN   Jealous.

LEO   Maybe. Yes.

DAN   Why didn't you say?

EMILY   **Paid for it.**
              Said I would but he insisted. His treat.

DAN   You need something
              You feel something
              You say it.
              You say it with you mouth
              Moving you mouth
              Like this
              Moving your tongue like
              LA LA LA LA LA
              Saying it.
              See?
              Like that.
              Communicate.

LEO   I know.

DAN   Not fuck someone else.

ANNA   **Where is he from?**

DAN	Is this a game?
EMILY	**Sorry?**
ANNA	**Do you know where he's from?**
DAN	Are you playing a game?
EMILY	**Anna.**
LEO	No.
ANNA	**London? Doncaster? The moon?**
LEO	No of course / I'm not.
ANNA	**Has he got any friends?** **Family?**
DAN	'wanted you to feel it too' What even is that?
ANNA	**Where are all his friends and family?** **Can you answer any of that?**
LEO	Lately it's been Feels like A lot of space Here Between us.
ANNA	**Don't know anything about him.** **Not really.**
LEO	I just don't know how to close it.
EMILY	**Did you want me to go alone?**
DAN	He was your idea.
ANNA	**A total fucking stranger**
DAN	It's your role-play It's your choice It's your game

ANNA	**Living here, living in our flat.**
DAN	Can't keep making up new rules then breaking them.
EMILY	**On my own.** **Would you have felt better?**
ANNA	**Maybe. Yes.** **In some fucked way yes maybe yes I think I** **would have.**
	,
	Sorry, I'm…
EMILY	**Can't you be happy someone was there?**
DAN	I don't want this.
EMILY	**He's been good.**
DAN	I don't want to play this game.
EMILY	**Supportive and understanding, and –**
LEO	Yes yes yes Okay good Because that's what I want. No more games. We can just Shut it all down
	I think stopping this with Al Taking a breath. I think that's going to really help.
EMILY	**We chose him.** **We wanted this.**
DAN	I don't want to do that.
LEO	What?
DAN	He likes me.

LEO   No he doesn't

DAN   We have a good time.

            He's interested in the things I'm interested in.

LEO   We pay him, Dan.
            That's why he likes us.
            We're paying him.

            ,

            He comes here because he's paid
            Usually by the hour usually
            Sometimes a set fee for the evening.

            ,

            It's a service.

ANNA   **Going to take some time off.**
            After the conference, I think.
            Be here. If you need me.

EMILY   **You're being silly.**

ANNA   **I want to.**

EMILY   **We need the money**
            Everything we can get right now.

ANNA   **Go on sabbatical.**
            I can do that.

EMILY   **Can we afford that?**
            Don't think we can afford that.

LEO   I didn't tell / you because –

DAN   I think you should go.

ANNA   **We've got savings.**

EMILY   **Not much.**

LEO   I'm telling you
            I'm being honest with you.

ANNA   **I've got savings.**

EMILY   **For the baby.**
             No.
             Don't want that.

DAN   I want you out.

LEO   No.

ANNA   **Okay**
             Well…

LEO   Let's talk.
             Figure it out.

ANNA   **I'll figure it out.**
             Work from home
             If they'll let me.

EMILY   **Don't need to.**

ANNA   **I want to.**

EMILY   **Okay.**

             I'd like that.

DAN   I don't want that now.

ANNA   **Good.**
             Me too.

DAN   Get out.

ANNA   **Come here.**

LEO   I live here.

             ,

             I live here, Dan.

             Where do you want me to go?

ANNA   **Will put in a request in the morning.**
             A couple months. They'll understand.
             Janine's been great.

Been asking about you.
Everyone really.
They know that we're…
That this…
That you come first now
Okay?

Yes. That'll work for us.
I'll be here, at my desk, here.
And if you need me,
If you need someone to help you,
I can be there.

EMILY   ,

Might want to ask Robert first.
Just make sure.

ANNA   ,

What?

EMILY   His university degree.
Most of its online now.

Might be a bit tight.
WiFi bandwidth and all that.

Just good to double check.

,

He does sit at that desk sometimes.

Sixteen

LEO *and* AL.

AL   How have you been?

            My nipples are out
            Sorry,
            Was just in the shower.
            Heard the doorbell and wrapped this round me.
            Hope you don't mind.

LEO   Why are you here?

AL   Bit abrupt.

LEO   Sorry I just
            Er

            Wasn't expecting to…

            Didn't know you would…

            Why are you / here?

AL   Is everything okay, Leo?

LEO   (*Shouting*.) Dan!

            (*To* AL.) Can you just get Dan, please.

AL   I don't think he wants to speak to you.

LEO   (*Shouting*.) It's Leo!

            (*To* AL.) We spoke on WhatsApp.

            (*Shouting*.) Dan, are you there?!

AL   Can't hear you from the shower.
            He's just jumped in.
            Likes to watch me shower first,
            Get himself off,
            Watch me shower and then
            After he comes
            He'll get in the shower and clean himself.
            You know what he's like.

            ,

Maybe you don't.

,

You never really knew what he liked.

LEO	Can I come in?
AL	I don't think that's a good idea.
LEO	Okay, Well.

I think that's a bit...

AL	?
LEO	It's not your flat.
AL	Here to pick up some last bits, yes?
LEO	Territorial.
AL	Hold on.

AL disappears.

LEO   Don't think you're entitled to –

Excuse me.

Hello?

Sorry but you can't just

Can you open the door, please?

Hello?

Dan?

Can you hear me?

AL reappears.

AL   Sorry.

We get a horrible draught if we keep the door open.
Is it just the one box?

Careful. It's heavy.
Your slow cooker is at the bottom.

	Is it all there? Can check if there's anything else?
LEO	He kicked me out because of you.
	,
	Because he found out.
AL	That's really nothing to do / with me.
LEO	I told him About our Financial Arrangement.
	I was so scared of losing him that I kept this thing This secret I kept it So that I wouldn't And then I lost him anyway.
AL	I don't know why you're telling me this.
LEO	And he made me feel bad. He made me feel really bad And rightly I felt Horrendous
	Look.
	I'm even still fucking… Blocked nose, When I talk about it.
	Anyway. Not now. Because Flash fucking forward Here you are.
AL	Leo
LEO	With him.

You.
The atomic bomb.

Paying for the grenade that blew us to pieces.
So I think I deserve some...
Spending all that time feeling shitty about myself
And really
He's just as bad now
Isn't he.

AL   You should go.

LEO   I think I'll just stay here
            And I'll wait, actually.

AL   Leo.

LEO   How much more time have you got left?
            What has he paid for?
            An hour? Two?
            The whole evening.
            I'll wait here.
            Until your time is up.

AL   Dan's not paying.

LEO   ,

            What?

AL   It's not an arrangement
            Any more.
            I live here.
            With Dan.
            Together.

LEO   ,

AL   ...

LEO   ,

AL   I'm sure we'll be in touch
            Over WhatsApp
            If we find anything else.

LEO	,
	Purple towel.
	,
	That's my towel.
AL	Oh. This?
	We share all the towels between us now.
	Dan isn't precious about whose towel is whose.
LEO	That one is mine. The purple one.
	,
	I'd like it.
	,
	I'd like to take that towel with me.
AL	You're making this harder than it needs to be. I don't think you really want that. Not really.
LEO	,
	I really want my towel.
AL	,
	Okay.
	,
	Shall I put it the box?
	There you go.
	,
	Happy?
	,
	Is there anything else, Leo?
	We get a horrible draught if we keep the door open.

Seventeen

ANNA *and* ROBERT.

ANNA	Don't expect you to move out straight away. Give you some time, of course To the end of the week. Find somewhere new.
ROBERT	Oh.
ANNA	Might be a bit tight. WiFi bandwidth and all that Once I start working from home
ROBERT	Baby isn't due for a couple months.
ANNA	We're ordering bits and bobs Cot, pushchair, et cetera. All arriving soon. Will be good, having some space.
ROBERT	Where?
ANNA	Sorry?
ROBERT	I don't have anywhere to go.
ANNA	Been having a look Just a gander What's on the market. Got a list of places that might work. Hopefully give you a head start.
ROBERT	Does Emily know about this?
ANNA	And most of your course is online now Isn't it? So you don't even need to be in the city.
ROBERT	She didn't say anything last night. Had a couple of beers on the sofa.
ANNA	Might find somewhere cheaper if you moved out a little further Might be better for you to move away.

ROBERT   ,

                I'm not sure I want to do that.

ANNA   ,

                Sorry?

ROBERT   I'm quite settled now.

ANNA   You'll move anyway
                When the baby comes.
                Now just a couple months earlier.

ROBERT   I assumed we would repurpose your office space.
                Put the baby in there.

ANNA   What?

ROBERT   Think I'll stay in my room.
                Quite like it now that it's painted.

ANNA   It's not...
                You don't pay for...
                We let you live here.

ROBERT   A mutually beneficial arrangement
                Works for everyone.

ANNA   Not me.

                Doesn't work for me.

ROBERT   ,

                It works for Emily.

ANNA   Want you to leave.

ROBERT   Wouldn't want to put Emily in the middle.

ANNA   Calling her.

ROBERT   I don't think so.

ANNA   Hear what she says.

ROBERT   You can try if you like.
                Won't pick up.

ANNA   ,

              What?

ROBERT   Won't have any signal.

              On the Tube.
              She'll be on the Tube now.

              ,

              Every day at this time she's on the Tube.
              Finishes work about…
              Ten minutes ago And now,
              For the next twenty-seven minutes,
              She's on the Tube.

              Did you know that?

              ,

              I live in your house I eat your food

              Your fiancée is carrying my baby.

              ,

              I think it's best to forget this conversation.
              Keep our arrangement as it is.
              Don't you?

              Maybe we should
              Have a *Men in Black* moment
              Boop.
              Erase All Memory
              And
              Forget all about this.

              ,

              Okay?

              Shall we do that?

              ,

              Yes. I think so.

              ,

Great.

I'll talk to Emily about repurposing the office.

She'll be off the Tube soon.

Eighteen

LEO *and* DAN.

DAN   Heard you moved back in with your mum.

LEO   Where did you hear that?

DAN   Nowhere.
           Just
           The office.

LEO   Is that going round the office?

DAN   Wouldn't read much into it.
           You know how it is.

LEO   Who in the office?

DAN   I don't have very long.

LEO   Was it Jane?

DAN   Jane?

LEO   Dyed her hair pink.
           Just the top bit.

DAN   Leo.

LEO   Like an iced gem.

DAN   I'm leaving.

LEO   ,

           Oh. Congratulations (?)

           Didn't know you'd applied for something.

DAN   Not the job.
           I am leaving the job but
           Because
           I'm *leaving* leaving.

           ,

           He wants to be closer to home.
           His home.

	Got a job near. We've decided to move up Together. I want to go too.
	We're moving in with his folks for a bit. Get our own place eventually.
LEO	Why are you telling me this?
DAN	I thought If you're still living with your mum You might want to stay in the flat?
	Not for free. I'd rent it to you. Cheaply.
LEO	Rent it to me?
DAN	A bit cheaper than if it was someone else.
LEO	Rent me my own flat?
DAN	I'm trying to be nice
LEO	Yeah, well Thank you, but No. Thank you.
DAN	Okay.
	,
	Just thought.
LEO	,
	I actually…
	There was a part of my brain that convinced itself you'd invited me here because
	That you were going to ask if I wanted
	Me and you.
	Again.
	Give it a go.

DAN	,
	Sorry.
LEO	When do you leave?
DAN	Today.
LEO	Right. Wow.
DAN	He's picking me up here.
LEO	What about work?
DAN	Gave my notice last month.
LEO	Have you found something?
DAN	Going to land and then just… see what's out there, I guess.
LEO	You don't have a job?
DAN	I have thought about this actually.
LEO	Leaving your flat Leaving your job for someone you've known half a minute.
DAN	Over a year now.
LEO	It's quite a lot for him to expect you to do that.
DAN	It was a mutual decision.
LEO	Won't walk into another one At your level Not with how things are at the moment.
DAN	I think I'm only still at this job because it worked for us.
	,
	Ready for something new.
	Think I've been ready for a while.
LEO	,
	Is it better?

With him?

,

No sorry don't answer that.

,

DAN   He listens to me.
        When we talk.
        When we're at dinner.
        When we watch a film.

LEO   Yes.

        ,

        Cute.
        Happy for you.

        ,

DAN   Let me know if you change your mind about the
        flat.

        A moment.

        Then,
        A spaceship lands.

        DAN *puts on a space helmet, gets in, and flies
        away.*

        LEO *watches him disappear into space.*

Nineteen

ANNA, EMILY, *and* ROBERT.

EMILY   Can someone turn out the lights?

ANNA   He'll start crying
             God
             Don't

EMILY   He'll be fine.

ROBERT   The lighter isn't…
             Ah.
             Here we go.

EMILY   Do you want me to /

ROBERT   Got it now.

ANNA   He's in the cot.

ROBERT   Is he asleep?
             Think / he's asleep.

EMILY   Probably /

ANNA   He's always asleep /

ROBERT   I'll get his bib

ANNA   He hasn't tried cake before.

ROBERT   Are we ready?

EMILY   One sec.
             Have you got the camera?

ANNA   This is big. Is it a tray bake?

ROBERT   It's flickering. Don't want the candle to

EMILY   Cover it with you hand.

ANNA   You bought a one-year-old a tray bake?
             How are we going to eat this?

ROBERT   There's a breeze.
             It keeps flickering.

EMILY   Ready?

ROBERT   Here.

EMILY   (*Starting to sing 'Happy Birthday'*.)
            Haaaaa…

            Guys!

            ROBERT *joins in*.

            ANNA *doesn't*.

EMILY/ROBERT

            Happy birthday to you
            Happy birthday to you
            Happy birthday baby Robert
            Happy birthday to you.

            They blow out the candle.

            Darkness.

            ANNA, *watching the baby*.

            A moment.

            Then,
            A small, green ALIEN *levitates out of the cot*.

            Mid-air, it turns to face ANNA.

            The ALIEN *smiles at her*.

            End.

A Nick Hern Book

This revised edition of *I Fucked You in My Spaceship* first published in Great Britain as a paperback original in 2023 by Nick Hern Books Limited, The Glasshouse, 49a Goldhawk Road, London W12 8QP

First published by Nick Hern Books in *Plays from VAULT 6* in 2023

I Fucked You in My Spaceship copyright © 2023 Louis Emmitt-Stern

Louis Emmitt-Stern has asserted his right to be identified as the author of this work

Cover artwork by Jess Reid

Designed and typeset by Nick Hern Books, London
Printed in Great Britain by Mimeo Ltd, Huntingdon, Cambridgeshire PE29 6XX

A CIP catalogue record for this book is available from the British Library

ISBN 978 1 83904 255 3

CAUTION All rights whatsoever in this play are strictly reserved. Requests to reproduce the text in whole or in part should be addressed to the publisher.

Amateur Performing Rights Applications for performance, including readings and excerpts, by amateurs in the English language throughout the world should be addressed to the Performing Rights Manager, Nick Hern Books, The Glasshouse, 49a Goldhawk Road, London W12 8QP, *tel* +44 (0)20 8749 4953, *email* rights@nickhernbooks.co.uk, except as follows:

Australia: ORiGiN Theatrical, Level 1, 213 Clarence Street, Sydney NSW 2000, *tel* +61 (2) 8514 5201, *email* enquiries@originmusic.com.au, *web* www.origintheatrical.com.au

New Zealand: Play Bureau, 20 Rua Street, Mangapapa, Gisborne 4010, *tel* +64 21 258 3998, *email* info@playbureau.com

United States of America and Canada: Berlin Associates, see details below

Professional Performing Rights Applications for performance by professionals in any medium and in any language throughout the world (and amateur and stock performances in the United States of America and Canada) should be addressed to Berlin Associates, 7 Tyers Gate, London SE1 3HX, *fax* +44 (0)20 7632 5296, *email* agents@berlinassociates.com

No performance of any kind may be given unless a licence has been obtained. Applications should be made before rehearsals begin. Publication of this play does not necessarily indicate its availability for performance.

www.nickhernbooks.co.uk/environmental-policy

www.nickhernbooks.co.uk

facebook.com/nickhernbooks

twitter.com/nickhernbooks